Mornings at the Cemetery

Mornings at the Cemetery
──────── A Collection of Haiku ────────

Deanna J. Woodall

RESOURCE *Publications* • Eugene, Oregon

MORNINGS AT THE CEMETERY
A Collection of Haiku

Copyright © 2025 Deanna J. Woodall. All rights reserved. Except for brief quotations in critical publications or reviews, no part of this book may be reproduced in any manner without prior written permission from the publisher. Write: Permissions, Wipf and Stock Publishers, 199 W. 8th Ave., Suite 3, Eugene, OR 97401.

Resource Publications
An Imprint of Wipf and Stock Publishers
199 W. 8th Ave., Suite 3
Eugene, OR 97401

www.wipfandstock.com

PAPERBACK ISBN: 979-8-3852-4827-8
HARDCOVER ISBN: 979-8-3852-4828-5
EBOOK ISBN: 979-8-3852-4829-2

VERSION NUMBER 09/24/25

Contents

Preface | vii
Introduction | ix
About Haiku | xi
About Sumi-e | xv

Early Reflections | 1

Spring | 63
Summer | 85
Autumn | 101
Winter | 119

Preface

Deanna Justine Woodall, a businesswoman in information technology before retiring, has traveled extensively worldwide and occasionally lived abroad before devoting herself to writing and artistic pursuits.

The sudden death of her beloved husband led to writing *Mornings at the Cemetery*, which is a collection of haiku. Using this poetic format, she conveyed her emotions. These poems were written by her over many months at the cemetery while she sat on a garden bench at his graveside.

At the cemetery, the author's long period of mourning and feelings of loss found a needed connection. Those visits during springtime, summer, autumn, and winter revealed the sounds of wildlife, the touch of the rain, the falling snow, flowers in bloom, and seeing others visiting graves. The cemetery gradually became a safe and peaceful place of remembrance and reflection for a long time. It was a community, which accepted mourning without judgement.

Introduction

This collection of haiku, in part, remembers morning visits at the cemetery. These poems give expression for the place where the author's beloved husband was buried. The many visits at the cemetery developed a connection, which gave relief from grief. The haiku collections were written on a garden bench at the graveside, revealing emotions and describing nature over the four seasons.

Her husband's sudden death was the force behind visits there. It continued a connection that refused to be separated by death. The selection of haiku gave the poet a unique format to express emotions and sometimes to send a message, or to share a moment captured in nature.

In the early visits at the cemetery, the author formed an acquaintance with the cemetery's surroundings. Many of the headstones recalled to her a view back in time, pronouncing political affiliations, religion, even love letters and poems engraved to read.

The early reflections at the cemetery are followed by seasonal reflections as the four seasons offer an opportunity to feel, to hear, and to see into this peaceful world, to capture a mood of springtime, summertime, autumn, and winter. There is beauty, sadness, longing, joy, and love in each season, conveyed through haiku.

About Haiku

Poetic expression in haiku requires a specific structure. Its poetic form is written in three lines, with seventeen syllables, giving 5-7-5 syllables respectively to each of those three lines. An example follows:

life is a journey
the path ahead is unknown
the moment is now

life	is	a	jour	ney
1	2	3	4	5

the	path	a	head	is	un	known
1	2	3	4	5	6	7

the	mo	ment	is	now
1	2	3	4	5

This haiku suggests to the reader that making a deliberate effort to focus now is the force you can harness to energize your life.

Another example suggests a universal truth.

        playful yearlings romp
      cold and hungry days ahead
          ignorance is bliss

play	ful	year	lings	romp
1	2	3	4	5

cold	and	hun	gry	days	a	head
1	2	3	4	5	6	7

ig	nor	ance	is	bliss
1	2	3	4	5

Lastly, heartfelt emotions can be conveyed about love of family, friendships, sadness, romance, and well wishes.

        life's hungry journey
    bring your love along the way
          it feeds everyone

life's	hun	gry	jour	ney
1	2	3	4	5

bring	your	love	a	long	the	way
1	2	3	4	5	6	7

it	feeds	eve	ry	one
1	2	3	4	5

light at tunnel's end
how long the journey for me
to find peace of mind

light	at	tun	nel's	end
1	2	3	4	5

how	long	the	jour	ney	for	me
1	2	3	4	5	6	7

to	find	peace	of	mind
1	2	3	4	5

two people in love
together forevermore
share wonders of life

two	peo	ple	in	love
1	2	3	4	5

to	ge	ther	for	ev	er	more
1	2	3	4	5	6	7

share	won	ders	of	life
1	2	3	4	5

Finally, in just seventeen syllables a haiku can convey a moment which caught our attention, and is to be remembered and shared.

Nota Bene: The poet used the Merriam Webster dictionary for syllabication.

About Sumi-e

The art of Japanese sumi-e often accompanies a haiku poem. It utilizes a technique of black ink brushstrokes onto white paper. This contrast in black and white sees equal partners as the accomplishment of the composition all together. Any sumi-e arrangement is completed with forceful concentration and meaningful brushstrokes to bring a pleasing accompaniment to a haiku.

Sometimes a symbolic message can be conveyed. For example,

To explain, this sumi-e depicts the force of wind as movement in a life force. Dark and light blossoms depict positive and negative elements. Buds are new growth which shows evolving life, bringing maturity against youth.

Sumi-e is not always complex in symbolism and composition. A pretty blossom in springtime or a bird on a leafy branch in summer can be just that simple.

Early Reflections

Life is a journey
The path ahead is unknown
The moment is now

Life's fleeting moments
Stories of many lives gone
At the cemetery

Death without warning
Fall off the edge of the Earth
Finding timeless space

A beating heart stops
The body gives up a soul
A spirit released

Shocking sudden death
We did not cry together
No chance for Goodbye

Ever lasting love,
Still that feeling in my heart
Does not separate

Struggling separation
Struggling for a connection
Visits to the graveside

Cemetery visits
The seasons have consoled me
Secrets to myself

I keep to myself
No one else can feel this sadness
Grief is forever

A place for the dead
Emotional bonds that remain
The burden of grief

Step by step alone
Pathways through the cemetery
history to life

Rainy morning visit
Melding the tears from my eyes
My sadness lingers

I cannot go away
Each day connects me to him
In the cemetery

I tell a few lies
My mourning is not over
Misery flows too deep

Miserable day
I cannot leave this cold bench
Waiting to connect

Where does lost love go?
I loathe this separation
I cannot touch you

Near one another now
Very subtle connections
Have developed

Keep it to myself
My wanderings near your grave
Find your neighbors

Harder to forgive
The life we lived together
Separated in Death

Alone without you
The new vision of myself
Struggles to survive

To confront a ghost
Willful imagination
Needs a helpful hand

The best years of my Life
Cradled in my Heart and Soul
Gone in an Instant

History is alive
Storytelling headstones reveal
A witness to life

My mind is in shock
My grieving heart still pains me
Yet, I am doing

What will I do now?
I cannot see a future
Working by myself

My eyes are burning
The salty tears cloud my sight
I can't see through them

So far from pleasure
Feeling pain of loneliness
Death extends its hand

No obvious signs
I try to understand death
How did this happen?

No comfort for me
Imagination finds me
A bitter moment

My heart is still true
It cannot be half empty
We were always one

Longing for the days
When we were both together
I remember then

I am here my love
Soft murmurs seem to reach me
Fill my mind with peace

Missing our marriage
Truly, I know it is done
Reason defies me

Missing our marriage
One more minute I yearn for
My sad fantasy

Can't rewind the past
What should have been done different?
Suffering regrets

I was not awake
Could I somehow be to blame
Could I have saved him?

My man was dying
It happened without me
Did he call to me?

Christmas without him
Makes a sad remembrance
Sitting at graveside

Suffering, deep guilt
I will never get answers
It would be very helpful

We had the very best
We earned it together
We were very grateful

We were so very close
The misery in losing him
Makes me feel in half

Eternal questions
The identity of life
Death will reveal all

My devotion to you
A marriage like no other love
Owns my heart and soul

Grateful for this love
Soul mates forge together
Two equals one of us

Our dreaming came true
I'm telling myself great times
No longer to share

Have a lot of friends
You may have many chances to play
Find a good playmate

We were good playmates
A life of work set us free
Freedom was money

Is help around me?
Alone on a graveyard bench
Hear the spirits sigh

Anger hides the tears
A heart with sadness suffers
You think no one knows

Deep water conceals
Below the turbulent waves
Memories of you

Sirens in the night
Awakens me to terror
Lights flash through the glass

Wind blown cemetery
Who here has deserted life?
Hear the spirits cry

Life can seem too long
Misery can scar a heart
You are not alone

Find comfort in tears
It is good to cry aloud
Someone may hear you

Echoes in the wind
Soft murmurs surrounding me
Give me peace of mind

Find comfort in tears
It is good to cry aloud
Someone may hear you

Life has been betrayed
All feelings triumph logic
Death has been embraced

Life has been betrayed
Death has been embraced
Angry souls are here

Anger hides the tears
A heart with sadness suffers
You think no one knows

When love turns to grief
Reluctant feelings shout out
Life faces sorrow

Acceptance of death
Passage to the other world
Time to rest in peace

Shadows at graveside
Darkness swallowing sunlight
All souls are restless

Presence of lost souls
Forever seeking moonlight
Find hope in the night

A magnetic pull
My broken heart always leads
To the cemetery

Life has been betrayed
Death has been embraced
Angry souls are here

Grief defies reason
All feelings triumph logic
Living suffers loss

Center of my life
My sadness which no one shares
Grounds my force of life

Sudden death tonight
Shocked to see my beloved
Death without warning

Powerful memory
No more splendor together
You lie before me

Horror at midnight
A shock to see my beloved
Seen without warning

Why did you leave me
Powerful memories hurt
The sadness lingers

I am here my love
Soft murmurs seem to reach me
Find my lonely heart

Struggles in living
Visit souls who are restless
No struggles in death

Here you are with me
Reaching into other worlds
Brings us together

A world beyond death
Transcendent imaginings
Still keeps us apart

Perception of death
An imaginary slumber
Allows connection

Center of my life
A soul mate forevermore
Gone in an instant

Imagination
A ghost is now my partner
Hidden world of souls

Graveside visiting
Secretive mournful feelings
Soothe a grieving heart

Grief is forever
So much time to mourn someone
Yet time is precious

Feeling the same way
Each and every season's change
Memories will last

Grieving nowadays
Finds spare patience among us
Find better friendships

Start looking for nests
Migratory birds find branches
Cemetery homesteads

In the midnight hour
A version of myself died
I am now alone

All souls buried here
In my imagination
Seem restless today

Two people in love
Found joy in each other's arms
Those moments are gone

Sharing all our dreams
Life snatched by cruel fate
Alone in a flash

Today sharing dreams
Life snatched by cruel fate
One partner grieving

Mourning suits a death
Celebration of lost life
Not my way of thought

Mourning defines death
Celebrating life lost
Angers the spirit

How could you leave me
Is anger filling my heart
Love has broken me

Grief's cruel burden
Mourning no one else can share
Suffering alone

A broken heart heals
The scarring remains tender
Live to love again

Given gift of life
Make every moment matter
Make it a mission

Occasional calls
Together a little while
The moment is ours

A very special man
Dealt a lucky hand in life
We grew together

Alone together
A lonely relationship
Cannot make a match

Life is a journey
The path ahead is unknown
The moment is now

Life's hungry journey
Bring your love along the way
It feeds everyone

Light at tunnel's end
How long the journey for me
To find peace of mind

Deep water conceals
Below the turbulent waves
Memories of you

Awake in the dark
Man conjectures how to hear
Answers in the wind

Presence of lost souls
Forever seeking moonlight
Find hope in the night

Life has been betrayed
Some reluctant souls are here
Death has been embraced

Another dawn breaks
The earth shelters everyone
Alone together

Acceptance of death
Passage to the other world
Time to rest in peace

When love turns to grief
Reluctant feelings shout out
Help is on the way

No one else can see
Hidden emotions struggle
Living life alone

Everyone in life
Mortality and losses
Bring us together

Don't forget to look
Living life and loving life
All for the taking

Alone together
A lonely relationship
Satisfies no one

Somewhere joy abounds
Reconnecting loving hearts
Let someone reach you

Tearful eyes reveal
You were the center of life
Gone in an instant

There's another world
There is a world of spirits
Hidden from ourselves

How could you leave me?
My anger has just been found
Where did it come from?

Care for another
Seek that generous exchange
Connect to someone

At the cemetery
Engraved name on a headstone
Is witness to life

Share intimately
Let your lover be your friend
Voices communicate

Am I Happy yet?
Searching for Peace
I have found Relief

Wake up a new day
Everyone has a story to tell
Do you want to share?

I love having life
But when all my strength is gone
Who is strong for me?

To hear and be heard
To listen and to speak aloud
Knowledge is power

Spring

Tender, young sparrows
Eager to leave their crowded nest
Will try to fly soon

Close the umbrella
The sunlight shines through the clouds
The ground is still wet

Springtime afternoon
Bright sunshine warms the garden
Flowers soon follow

Wandering alone
Noisy cemetery bird life
Lets me know my place

Today's cool, fresh air
Touches all of my senses
I am feeling alive

Playful everyday
Nature keeps changing its mind
Follows no leader

Thirsty garden plants
Soft rain pleasing the flowers
Springtime has arrived

Quiet cemetery
Temperamental nestlings
Awakening silence

Human emotions
Searching the cemetery
Connections are made

Grappling with death
Seeking a true connection
Can't be found in life

Cemetery has a canvas
Gravestones paint its history
For all to explore

Creative impulses
Finding haiku expressions
For poetic release

Long cemetery walks
Reading history on gravestones
Time stands still for them

Evenings darkened light
A golden horizon fades
The nestlings find sleep

Noisy nestlings screech
Empty bellies want filling
Their voices are heard

Early dawn in springtime
A few patches of frost melts
Young tree buds unfurl

Evening spring rain
Will feed the hungry earth
The flowers bloom

A graceful dogwood
Proud of its springtime blossoms
Shows off its beauty

Playful yearlings romp
Cold and hungry days ahead
Ignorance is bliss

Brown and black starling
Looking for a true lover
Preens his fine feathers

Have you felt the Spring?
Do you know the touch of Love?
Why don't you share it?

Silken spider webs
Deserted for a season
Warm the fledglings nest

Life can seem too long
Misery can scar a heart
You are not alone

Two people in love
Together forever more
Share wonders of life

Hear the spirits cry
Remembrance
The scent of springtime

Evening's darkened light
A golden horizon fades
The nestlings find sleep

Noisy nestling screech
Empty bellies want filling
Their voices are heard

Early dawn in springtime
A few patches of frost melt
Young tree buds unfurl

Chirping chickadees
Announce their new hatchlings
Garden birds listen

Migratory birds
Land here for just a season
Find a nesting place

Charming chickadee
Now seeking a territory
Sings its famous song

Early spring raindrops
It is now time for new growth
Feed the hungry earth

Chattering lovebirds
Complaints are getting louder
No compromise yet

Sunshine getting warm
Sleepy, sparrows, awaken
Mist rises from the grass

Looking for a mate
Flirting is confirmation
A match may be made

Thirsty gardens wait
April rain nourishes flowers
Springtime remembers

Summer

Soaking morning rain
Makes sounds upon the gravestones
Washing dust away

Heavy clouds of fog
Linger low in the morning
Dawn shining through it

Shimmering flat moon
Moves across the sapphire sky
Too quick to capture

The threatening rain
Foraging birds do not stop
Dark clouds drift away

Busy buzzing bees
Too busy to bother with me
Gathering nectar

Pretty dragonflies
Drinking pearls of dewdrops
Rest upon a leaf

A graceful willow
Twilight in the rain
Time to leave my bench

Nectar laden bees
Finally flying homeward
The hive must be fed

Wandering barefoot
Cool grass wet between my toes
Cemetery secrets

We will meet again
Flowers covering your grave
Will warm your casket

Cheerful sparrow's songs
Tells a story of family
Flocking together

Start looking for nests
Migratory birds find branches
Cemetery homesteads

Consider beauty
The proud cemetery grounds
Look and you shall see

Chattering lovebirds
Complaints are getting louder
No compromises yet

Sunshine getting warm
Sleepy sparrows awaken
Mist rises from the grass

Soaking morning rain
Makes sounds upon the gravestones
Washing dust away

Vanishing summer
Evening comes sooner
Welcome cool night

A floral bouquet
At the graveside with no card
Must be a mistake

Drops of rain scatter
Cool and soft upon my face
Washes tears away

Rain drizzles down
See the headstones glistening
Death is honored

The scent of flowers
The sounds of chattering birds
Squirrels chase each other

Wind in the willow
Its graceful branches swaying
Shade moves side to side

Time to cut the thread
When tears become memories
Heartache is finished

Rainbows in daylight
Has darkness no such beauty?
Welcome silver moon!

Take a bite of life?
Much fruit is not ripe today
Can you pick the prime?

Murky brown pond
Alive with bubbling scum
Larvae grow until . . .

Better luck next time
Brokenhearted butterflies
Can't defy the wind

A long august day
Brilliant sunshine seems endless
Welcome shading clouds

Vanishing summer
Welcoming cooler mornings
Autumn is coming

Autumn

Evening crickets sing
Searching for a mate to love
Early autumn dusk

Autumn chilly rain
Candle light against the glass
Reflections, dancing

Endless autumn rain
No wild birds flying around
Grooming, wet feathers

Abundant acorns fall
Cemetery's ground is covered
Feasting squirrels delight

Windy afternoon
Golden leaves carpet the ground
Autumn has arrived

Dusky evening light
Lonely spirits beckon souls
A silent meeting

Tied to misery
What does tomorrow look like?
Cut the thread that binds

Sparrow in the oak
Complaining to the squirrel
Feasting by himself

A lovely sunset
Golden light frames the gravestones
A moment of peace

Last frost of autumn
Icy shimmer on the headstones
Beetles bury deep

Chilling autumn rain
Harbinger of morning frost
Making cold headstones

Cool and powerful
Autumn morning winds arrive
Forcing leaves to fall

A few telling signs
Flowers laid on marked graves
Lovers remember

Chilly autumn dusk
Daylight fades too quickly
Shadows find their place

Wild geese fly above
Goslings soft down gone away
Follow their leader

Noisy starlings flock
Alight on the tallest trees
Resting for awhile

Neighboring headstones
Engraving tells a history
Getting to know them

Golden foliage
The saw tooth oak's acorns falls
Squirrels are feasting

Frosty sunflowers
Glistening in the sunlight
Autumn fades away

Early autumn heat
Lazy birds and tired bugs
Find peace in the shade

Echoes in the wind
A feeling, which surrounds me
Gives me peace of mind

Shadows at graveside
Brings light into the darkness
All souls are restless

Autumn chilly rain
Candlelight against the glass
Reflections dancing

Reflect on the past
You cannot relive your life
Your life is this day

Harvest moon shines down
Silver fingertips surround
Touch a yearling's heart

Cannot make a match
Changing your life from within
Hear the fateful call

Thanksgiving dinner
An empty seat is honored
Alone with others

Chilly autumn day
Flickering candlelight dancing
Against the window panes

Soaking morning rain
Makes sounds upon the gravestones
Washing dust away

Wild geese flying high
Goslings, soft down, gone away
Follow their leader

Abundant acorns
Falling from the sawtooth oak
Feed the hungry squirrels

Winter

Familiar pathway
'The frozen grass has yielded
Visits remembered

Snow-white blanket
Covers cemetery graves
Winter wonderland

Wild wind tonight
Moving clouds across the moon
Scatters silver beams

Alas life must end
A soul rises to heaven
Our love stays with us

Separate headstones
Long shadows touching gravesides
A fleeting greeting

Winter snowflakes fall
Dressing silver white gravestones
A sadness lingers

Visiting the graves
Cemetery souls are family
Welcome everyone

I must walk away
Visiting today is done
Sadness trails me home

Awful chilly day
Sitting on a garden bench
Fond memories warm

Promise is change
Old paths are not a journey
Embrace a new life

My grief is forever
A love connection is here
Stay a while longer

Wearing my old boots
My cap covers my cold ears
Memories warm me

Weather is in flux
Seasons after seasons change
Always a surprise

A place for a wreath
A remembrance of life
Marking the graveside

Powerful feelings
Lonely days are forever
Mourning never leaves me

Coming and going
Winter footprints in soft snow
Visiting the grave

Familiar pathway
The frozen grass has yielded
Visits remembered

Razzle dazzle night
Fireworks light the midnight sky
The new year arrives

Communication
Center point of my searching
Pauses at graveside

Throughout the year
Four seasons have come and gone
The cemetery remains

A winter garden
Wreaths fade upon the graves
Blankets the beloved

Dark and stormy night
All souls are restless this evening
Find peace in getting light

A chilly morning
Silvery bushes light with frost
Foretelling winter

Windblown cemetery
Who here has deserted life?
Hear the spirits cry

Freezing midnight rain
Brings icy frozen morning
A glistening glaze

Beneath the cold earth
The living are above you
Prayer finds a soul

When love turns to grief
Reluctant feelings flow out
Life faces sorrow

Footprints in soft snow
Walking back from the graveside
Coming and going

Partly cloudy day
Those moments were ours to share
My bench is warmer

Freezing midnight rain
Visits as we are asleep
Winter wonderland

www.ingramcontent.com/pod-product-compliance
Lightning Source LLC
Chambersburg PA
CBHW071725090426
42738CB00009B/1885